Table of Contents
Phonics
Level 4

Review of Short Vowels

Hi! I'm Buddy Bear. I will help you learn many vowel rules.

Rule: In a short vowel word, with the vowel between two consonants, the vowel is usually short.

Say the name of each picture. Circle the pictures which have the same short vowel.

ŭ

ă

ĕ

ĭ

ŏ

ŭ

Review of Short Vowels

Circle each picture's name.
Write the word on the line.

crib (crab)	shop ∞ ship
crab	_____
sock sick	lost list
_____	_____
wag wig	gum gem
_____	_____
jet net	well wall
_____	_____
hit hat	cut cat
_____	_____

Say the name of each picture. Read each sentence. Write the missing short vowel word.

1. Pull the <u>tab</u> on the can.

tub
tab

2. Dad is a very tall _____ .

men
man

3. Grandpa forgot to get his _____ .

hit
hat

4. My _____ got hurt in the game.

lag
leg

5. I sleep on a _____ at camp.

cot
cat

6. My doctor gave me a _____ .

pill
hill

7. My sister has a pet _____ .

bag
bug

Review of Long Vowels

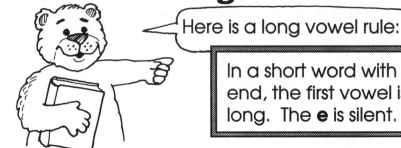

Here is a long vowel rule:

In a short word with **e** at the end, the first vowel is usually long. The **e** is silent.

Say the name of each picture. Circle the long vowel you hear.

ā ē ī   ō ū ā   ē ī ō

ū ā ē   ī ō ū   ā ē ī

ō ū ā   ē ī ō   ū ā ē

Find the hidden name of each picture. Write the word. Circle the long vowel you hear.

b l m s m i l e p t

s m i l e

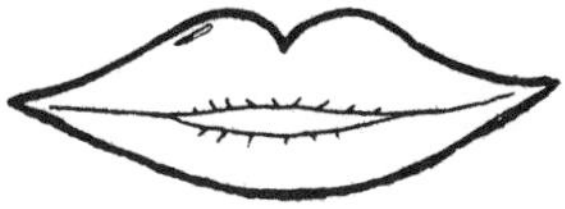

s h e e p l t m n

_____

b c a m p l a k e l s

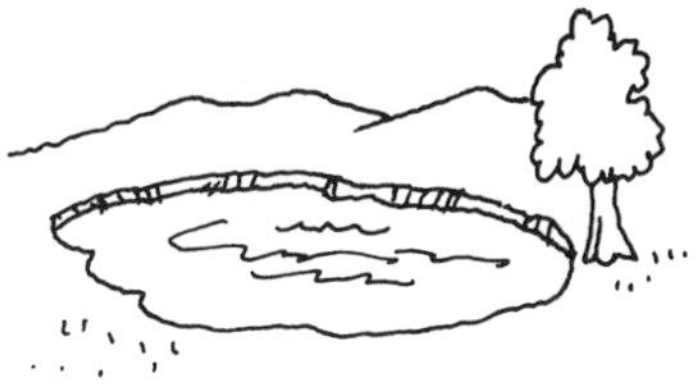

_____

c p l a o m r o p e t p

_____

t y l o s t u b e p r k

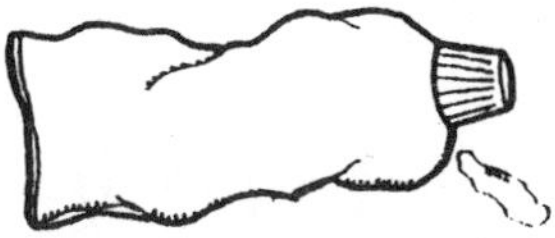

_____

m k i t e n r l e t d n r

_____

Review of Long Vowels

Work the long vowel crossword puzzles.

Across

1. You do this off of a board.

Down

2. 10 cents

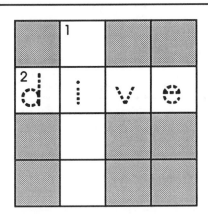

Across

1. You put ice cream in it.

Down

2. A dog likes it.

Across

1. You play it.

Down

2. Long hair on horse's neck

Say the words. Write the word which goes with each picture.

can

cane

can

robe

rob

pine

pin

cut

cute

Double Vowels ai and ay

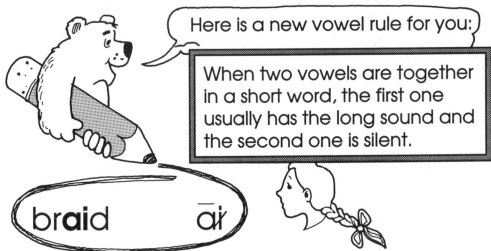

Here is a new vowel rule for you:

When two vowels are together in a short word, the first one usually has the long sound and the second one is silent.

braid   ai

Trace the words. Say the words. Circle the words with the **ai** that rhyme.

rain

faint

paid

tray āy

Choose the correct word and fill in the oval.
Write the word in the blank.

Please _pay_ first.	⬤ pay ◯ say ◯ day
_____ in the yard.	◯ Hay ◯ Play ◯ Bay
_____ your name.	◯ Day ◯ Pay ◯ Say
_____ I go too?	◯ Clay ◯ May ◯ Tray
Mules eat _____ .	◯ hay ◯ play ◯ stay

Double Vowels ee, ea, oa

cōat   ōa̸

bēads   ēa̸

shēep   ee̸

Read the words in the box below. Write the words in the sentences.

need	heat	soap

1. Wash your hands with _____ .

2. Do you _____ lunch money?

3. The stove makes _____ .

Read the words. Cut them out. Paste them in the sentences on page 13.

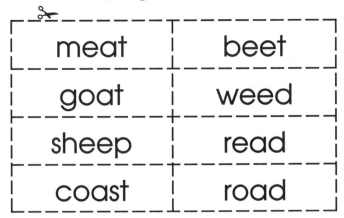

meat	beet
goat	weed
sheep	read
coast	road

1. My dog likes to eat a lot of
[   ] .

2. Keep your eyes on the [   ]
while driving.

3. The flower bed doesn't have one
[   ] .

4. Will you [   ] a story to your
sister?

5. My skin was as red as a [   ] .

6. That [   ] has long horns.

7. A [   ] gives us wool.

8. I will [   ] down the hill on my
bike.

Irregular Long Vowel igh(ī)

You are understanding the rules just fine. Here are two more.

The vowel **i** is long when followed by silent **gh**.

ni**gh**t

i**gh**

Read the words in the box. Write them in the sentences.

right	high	fight
bright	sight	light

1. Turn on a ___light___ .

2. The boys had a _____ .

3. My new kite went very _____ .

4. Glasses make my _____ better.

5. I write with my _____ hand.

6. The sun is _____ .

In a short word without the other vowels, **y** usually makes the long $\bar{i}$ sound.

Circle each picture's name.
Write the word under each picture.

(cry) spy	by dry
cry	_____
pry why	shy sky
_____	_____
my fly	fry fly
_____	_____
by spy	shy fry
_____	_____

Review

Y is a tricky letter. Here is another rule about a sound it makes.

The letters **y** or **ey** at the end of a two-syllable word usually make the long **e** sound.

Draw a line from each word to the correct picture.

bunny •

puppy •

money •

jelly •

pony •

honey •

twenty •

monkey •

Circle the word that goes with the picture.
Write the word.

(puppy) cry	pry cloudy
puppy	____
pony monkey	my twenty
____	____
jelly by	shy berry
____	____
baby try	money happy
____	____

Schwa Sound

Your next sound is called the **schwa**.

Any of the vowels **a**, **e**, **i**, **o** or **u** can make the **schwa** sound.

lem**o**n   o = ∂

bush**e**l   e = ∂

Circle the vowel which stands for the **schwa** sound (∂) in the word.

canoe	a e i o u	cabin	a e i o u
dragon	a e i o u	woman	a e i o u
balloon	a e i o u	zebra	a e i o u

(canoe: a is circled)

Print **a, e, i, o, u** to show which letter stands for the schwa sound (ə) as in **the**.

seven

salad

robin

circus

pilot

wagon

camel

barrel

walrus

bacon

R-Controlled Vowel ar ✓

Are you ready to start something new? Now, we're going to work on the r-controlled vowels.

> When a vowel is followed by the consonant **r**, it makes a new sound.

st**ar**   ar

Write **ar** on the line in each word. Draw a line to the correct picture.

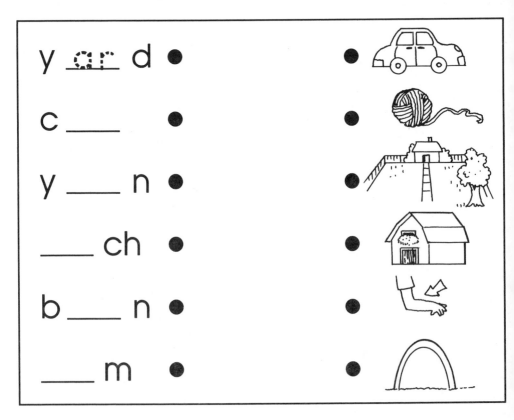

y _ar_ d •

c ___ •

y ___ n •

___ ch •

b ___ n •

___ m •

Say the words in the word bank. Use the words in the sentences.

scarf	cart	farm	card
dart	park	barn	hard

1. I sent you a pretty _____ .

2. We play on swings in the _____ .

3. Wrap the _____ around your

   neck.

4. The little _____ was pulled by a

   donkey.

5. Grandpa grows corn on his _____ .

6. The horses live in a _____ .

7. Throw the _____ at the cork board.

8. It is _____ to be good.

R-Controlled Vowel or

Write **or** in the box if you hear the **or** sound in the word.

Write **or** in the blanks. Say the words in the box.
Write the words in sentences.

f _or_ t	h ___ n	t ___ n
n ___ th	st ___ m	f ___ k

1. Steve ate his soup with his _____ !

2. The soldier went into the __fort__ .

3. A _____ came suddenly and

    the rain fell.

4. The _____ went "Honk!"

5. I went _____ by using my

    compass.

6. The sleeve on my shirt was _____ .

R-Controlled Vowels or, ar

Say the name of each picture. Circle the word.
Then, circle a word that rhymes with it.

	horn hot corn		cork pork hope
	car rag jar		thorn socks born
	far star mat		pat farm harm
	stork fox fork		yarn barn tan
	tab card yard		porch torch cot

Read the clues. Write the words in the puzzle.

mark	farm	pork	dart
card	harm	porch	

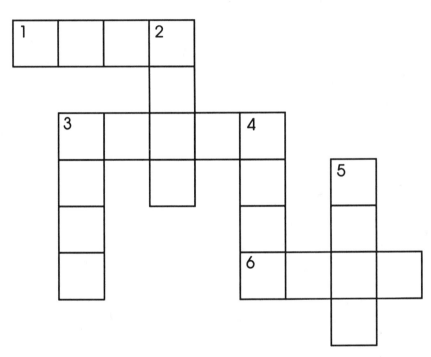

Down

2. throw it
3. We eat _____ from a pig.
4. to hurt
5. grow crops on it

Across

1. a birthday _____
3. around the door
6. make it with pencil

R-Controlled Vowel er

fern   er

Write **er** in the space in the words. Match the words to the pictures.

cl __er__ k   •   •

g ___ m   •   •

p ___ ch   •   •

lett ___   •   •

rul ___   •   •

tig ___   •   •

hamm ___   •   •

s ___ ve   •   •

f ___ n   •   •

Write the **er** words from page 26 in the sentences.

1. Use my __ruler__ to draw a line.

2. I wrote a _____ to my grandmother.

3. My parrot sits on his _____ .

4. The _____ has gold and black stripes.

5. Hit the nail with the _____ .

6. _____ treats to your guest first.

7. A _____ makes you sick.

8. I gave money to the store _____ .

9. We have a green _____ on the porch.

R-Controlled Vowel ir

These **ir** words have the same vowel sound as **er**, but they are always spelled **ir**.

shirt   ir

Write **ir** in the blanks. Cut out the words. Glue them beside the pictures below and on page 29.

1.	whirl
2.	

b ___ d	sh ___ t	th ___ sty
f ___ st	ch ___ p	d ___ t
th ___ d	th ___ ty	st ___
g ___ l	sk ___ t	wh ir l

R-Controlled Vowel ur

The sound made by **ur** is the same as **er** and **ir**.

purse   ur

Write **ur** in the blanks of these words.

b __ur__ n   s ___ e   f ___

t ___ tle   ch ___ ch   c ___ b

t ___ n   c ___ l   h ___ t

p ___ se

Draw a picture to go with each word.

burn	church	turtle

Write the **ur** words from page 30 in these sentences.

1. Fire can __burn__ you.

2. Mother put her money in her

   _____ .

3. The car was parked close to the

   _____ .

4. The _____ walks very slowly.

5. I am _____ I met you earlier.

6. The rain will make my hair _____ .

7. The cat has black _____ .

8. _____ right here.

9. Don't _____ yourself.

10. We pray at _____ .

Review R- Controlled Vowels

The letters **er**, **ir** and **ur** have the same sound.

fe**r**n ✓ er

g**ir**l ✓ ir

c**ur**l ✓ ur

Circle the name of each picture. Color the box below the picture showing the sound.

	(church) burn purr			farmer hammer tiger	
er	ir	**ur**	er	ir	ur
	skirt shirt dirt			burn purse sure	
er	ir	ur	er	ir	ur

	purse turkey fur			ruler serve germ	
er	ir	ur	er	ir	ur
	shirt girl chirp			herd jerk letter	
er	ir	ur	er	ir	ur
	skirt first third			hammer tiger ruler	
er	ir	ur	er	ir	ur
	hammer fern clerk			bird first girl	
er	ir	ur	er	ir	ur

Vowel Digraph oo

A new sound for you to remember today!

The letters **oo** in a word usually represent **oo** in moon (**ü**) or **oo** in book (**ü**).

moon   oo (ü)

Say the name of each picture. Circle the word.
Then, circle a word that rhymes with it.

	spoon		turn
	noon		zoo
	to	FEEDING TIME	too
	turtle		stool
	goose		duck
	moose		pool
	rule		moon
	broom		soon
	room		sky

Match these rhyming **oo** (ü) words.

1. moon •   • moo
2. shoot •   • spoon
3. too •   • boot
4. soon •   • moose
5. tooth •   • noon
6. cool •   • booth
7. goose •   • tool
8. boom •   • groom
9. pool •   • drool
10. zoo •   • stool
11. fool •   • boo

Vowel Digraph oo (ü)

The second sound made by **oo** is the sound heard in b**oo**k (ü).

f**er**n   er

Write **oo** in the blanks in the words. Say the words. Write the words under the correct pictures on page 37.

h oo d	w __ d
b __ k	cr __ ked
c __ k	w __ l
br __ k	f __ tball
st __ d	t __ k
h __ k	sh __ k
f __ t	g __ d

Tutor's Guide

This Tutor's Guide contains answer keys for Phonics Level 4. Pull it out from the book to use as a guide.

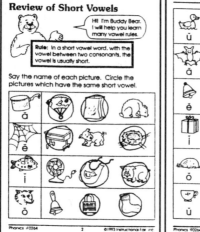

Review of Short Vowels

Hi! I'm Buddy Bear. I will help you learn many vowel rules.

Rule: In a short vowel word, with the vowel between two consonants, the vowel is usually short.

Say the name of each picture. Circle the pictures which have the same short vowel.

ă
ĕ
ĭ

ŭ
ă
ĕ
ĭ
ŏ
ŭ

Review of Short Vowels

Circle each picture's name. Write the word on the line.

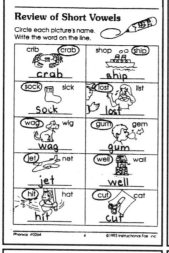

crib (**crab**)   **crab**
shop (**ship**)   **ship**
(**sock**) sick   **sock**
(**lost**) list   **lost**
(**wag**) wig   **wag**
(**gum**) gem   **gum**
(**jet**) net   **jet**
(**well**) wall   **well**
(**hit**) hat   **hit**
(**cut**) cat   **cut**

Say the name of each picture. Read each sentence. Write the missing short vowel word.

1. Pull the **tab** on the can. — tub / tab
2. Dad is a very tall **man**. — men / man
3. Grandpa forgot to get his **hat**. — hit / hat
4. My **leg** got hurt in the game. — lag / leg
5. I sleep on a **cot** at camp. — cot / cat
6. My doctor gave me a **pill**. — pill / hill
7. My sister has a pet **bug**. — bag / bug

Review of Long Vowels

Here is a long vowel rule:

In a short word with **e** at the end, the first vowel is usually long. The **e** is silent.

Say the name of each picture. Circle the long vowel you hear.

ā (ē) ī | (ō) ū ā | (ē) ī ō
(ū) ā ē | ī (ō) ū | (ā) ē ī
(ō) ū ā | ī ō (ū) | (ā) ē ī

Find the hidden name of each picture. Write the word. Circle the long vowel you hear.

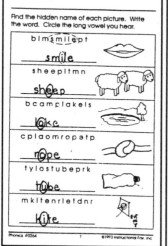

b l m s **smile** p t — **sm(i)le**
sheep l t m n — **sh(ee)p**
b c a m **lake** s — **l(a)ke**
c p l a o m **rope** a t p — **r(o)pe**
t y l o s **tube** p r k — **t(u)be**
m k l t e n r l e **kite** d n r — **k(i)te**

Review of Long Vowels

Work the long vowel crossword puzzles.

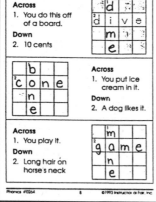

Across
1. You do this off of a board.
Down
2. 10 cents

```
    d
d  i  v  e
   m
   e
```

Across
1. You put ice cream in it.
Down
2. A dog likes it.

```
    b
c  o  n  e
   n
   e
```

Across
1. You play it.
Down
2. Long hair on horse's neck

```
      m
   g  a  m  e
      n
      e
```

Say the words. Write the word which goes with each picture.

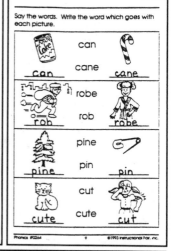

can — **can** | cane — **cane**
rob — **rob** | robe — **robe**
pine — **pine** | pin — **pin**
cut — **cut** | cute — **cute**

Double Vowels ai and ay

Here is a new vowel rule for you:

When two vowels are together in a short word, the first one usually has the long sound and the second one is silent.

braid āī

Trace the words. Say the words. Circle the words with the **ai** that rhyme.

rain
faint
paid

---

tray āy

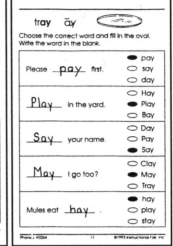

Choose the correct word and fill in the oval. Write the word in the blank.

Please **pay** first.	● pay / ○ say / ○ day
Play in the yard.	○ Hay / ● Play / ○ Bay
Say your name.	○ Day / ○ Pay / ● Say
May I go too?	○ Clay / ● May / ○ Tray
Mules eat **hay**.	● hay / ○ play / ○ stay

Double Vowels ee, ea, oa

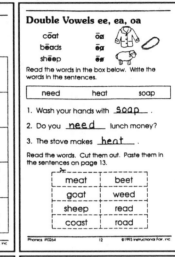

coat ōā
beads ēā
sheep ēē

Read the words in the box below. Write the words in the sentences.

| need | heat | soap |

1. Wash your hands with **soap**.
2. Do you **need** lunch money?
3. The stove makes **heat**.

Read the words. Cut them out. Paste them in the sentences on page 13.

meat	beet
goat	weed
sheep	read
coast	road

---

1. My dog likes to eat a lot of **meat**.
2. Keep your eyes on the **road** while driving.
3. The flower bed doesn't have one **weed**.
4. Will you **read** a story to your sister?
5. My skin was as red as a **beet**.
6. That **goat** has long horns.
7. A **sheep** gives us wool.
8. I will **coast** down the hill on my bike.

Irregular Long Vowel igh(ī)

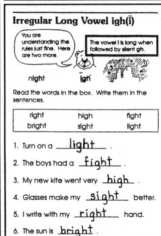

You are understanding the rules just fine. Here are two more.

The vowel i is long when followed by silent gh.

night igh

Read the words in the box. Write them in the sentences.

| right | high | fight |
| bright | sight | light |

1. Turn on a **light**.
2. The boys had a **fight**.
3. My new kite went very **high**.
4. Glasses make my **sight** better.
5. I write with my **right** hand.
6. The sun is **bright**.

In a short word without the other vowels, y usually makes the long i sound.

Circle each picture's name. Write the word under each picture.

cry / spy — **cry**
by / dry — **dry**
pry / why — **pry**
shy / sky — **sky**
my / fly — **fly**
fry / fly — **fry**
by / spy — **spy**
shy / fry — **shy**

Review

Y is a tricky letter. Here is another rule about a sound it makes.

The letters y or ey at the end of a two-syllable word usually make the long e sound.

Draw a line from each word to the correct picture.

bunny
puppy
money
jelly
pony
honey
twenty
monkey

Circle the word that goes with the picture. Write the word.

puppy / cry — **puppy**
pry / cloudy — **pry**
pony / monkey — **monkey**
my / twenty — **twenty**
jelly / by — **jelly**
shy / berry — **berry**
baby / try — **baby**
money / happy — **money**

Schwa Sound

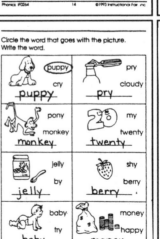

Your next sound is called the schwa.

Any of the vowels a, e, i, o or u can make the schwa sound.

lemon   o = ə
bushel   e = ə

Circle the vowel which stands for the **schwa** sound (ə) in the word.

canoe — a / o / u
cabin — a / i / u
dragon — a / o / u
woman — a / o / u
balloon — a / o / u
zebra — a / e / i / u

Panel 1 (top-left)

Print a, e, i, o, u to show which letter stands for the schwa sound (ə) as in the.

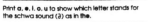

seven	e	salad	a
robin	i	circus	u
pilot	o	wagon	o
camel	e	barrel	e
walrus	u	bacon	o

Phonics IF0264   19   ©1993 Instructional Fair, Inc.

Panel 2 (top-middle)

R-Controlled Vowel ar

Are you ready to start something new? Now, we're going to work on the r-controlled vowels.

When a vowel is followed by the consonant r, it makes a new sound.

star   ar

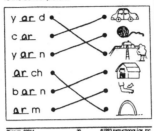

Write ar on the line in each word. Draw a line to the correct picture.

y ar d
c ar
y ar n
ar ch
b ar n
ar m

Phonics IF0264   20   ©1993 Instructional Fair, Inc.

Panel 3 (top-right)

Say the words in the word bank. Use the words in the sentences.

| scarf | cart | farm | card |
| dart | park | barn | hard |

1. I sent you a pretty **card** .
2. We play on swings in the **park** .
3. Wrap the **scarf** around your neck.
4. The little **cart** was pulled by a donkey.
5. Grandpa grows corn on his **farm** .
6. The horses live in a **barn** .
7. Throw the **dart** at the cork board.
8. It is **hard** to be good.

Phonics IF0264   21   ©1993 Instructional Fair, Inc.

Panel 4 (middle-left)

R-Controlled Vowel or

Write or in the box if you hear the or sound in the word.

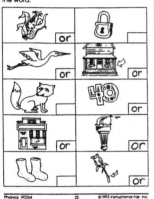

Phonics IF0264   22   ©1993 Instructional Fair, Inc.

Panel 5 (middle-middle)

Write or in the blanks. Say the words in the box. Write the words in sentences.

| f or t | h or n | t or n |
| n or th | st or m | f or k |

1. Steve ate his soup with his **fork** !
2. The soldier went into the **fort** .
3. A **storm** came suddenly and the rain fell.
4. The **horn** went "Honk!"
5. I went **north** by using my compass.
6. The sleeve on my shirt was **torn** .

Phonics IF0264   23   ©1993 Instructional Fair, Inc.

Panel 6 (middle-right)

R-Controlled Vowels or, ar

Say the name of each picture. Circle the word. Then, circle a word that rhymes with it.

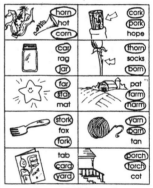

horn / hot / corn	cork / pork / hope
car / rag / jar	thorn / socks / born
far / star / mat	pat / farm / harm
stork / fox / fork	yam / barn / tan
tab / card / yard	porch / torch / cot

Phonics IF0264   24   ©1993 Instructional Fair, Inc.

Panel 7 (bottom-left)

Read the clues. Write the words in the puzzle.

| mark | farm | pork | dart |
| card | harm | porch | |

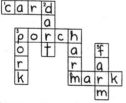

Down
2. throw it
3. We eat _____ from a pig.
4. to hurt
5. grow crops on it

Across
1. a birthday _____
3. around the door
6. make it with pencil

Phonics IF0264   25   ©1993 Instructional Fair, Inc.

Panel 8 (bottom-middle)

R-Controlled Vowel er

fern   er

Write er in the space in the words. Match the words to the pictures.

cl er k
g er m
p er ch
lett er
rul er
tig er
hamm er
s er ve
f er n

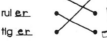

Phonics IF0264   26   ©1993 Instructional Fair, Inc.

Panel 9 (bottom-right)

Write the er words from page 26 in the sentences.

1. Use my **ruler** to draw a line.
2. I wrote a **letter** to my grandmother.
3. My parrot sits on his **perch** .
4. The **tiger** has gold and black stripes.
5. Hit the nail with the **hammer** .
6. **Serve** treats to your guest first.
7. A **germ** makes you sick.
8. I gave money to the store **clerk** .
9. We have a green **fern** on the porch.

Phonics IF0264   27   ©1993 Instructional Fair, Inc.

R-Controlled Vowel ir

These ir words have the same vowel sound as er, but they are always spelled ir.

shirt   ir

Write ir in the blanks. Cut out the words. Glue them beside the pictures below and on page 29.

| 1. | whirl |
| 2. | |

b __ir__ d	sh __ir__ t	th __ir__ sty
f __ir__ st	ch __ir__ p	d __ir__ t
th __ir__ d	th __ir__ ty	st __ir__
g __ir__ l	sk __ir__ t	wh __ir__ l

Phonics IF0264   28   ©1993 Instructional Fair, Inc.

3.	thirsty
4.	dirt
5.	girl
6.	third
7.	first
8.	shirt
9.	stir
10.	thirty
11.	skirt
12.	chirp

Phonics IF0264   29   ©1993 Instructional Fair, Inc.

R-Controlled Vowel ur

The sound made by ur is the same as er and ir.

purse   ur

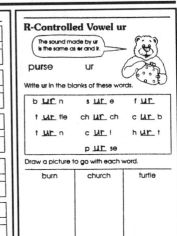

Write ur in the blanks of these words.

b __ur__ n	s __ur__ e	f __ur__
t __ur__ tle	ch __ur__ ch	c __ur__ b
t __ur__ n	c __ur__ l	h __ur__ t
	p __ur__ se	

Draw a picture to go with each word.

burn	church	turtle

Phonics IF0264   30   ©1993 Instructional Fair, Inc.

Write the ur words from page 30 in these sentences.

1. Fire can **burn** you.

2. Mother put her money in her **purse**.

3. The car was parked close to the **curb**.

4. The **turtle** walks very slowly.

5. I am **sure** I met you earlier.

6. The rain will make my hair **curl**.

7. The cat has black **fur**.

8. **Turn** right here.

9. Don't **burn** yourself.

10. We pray at **church**.

Phonics IF0264   31   ©1993 Instructional Fair, Inc.

Review R- Controlled Vowels

The letters er, ir and ur have the same sound.

fern   er
girl   ir
curl   ur

Circle the name of each picture. Color the box below the picture showing the sound.

| church / burn / purr | farmer / hammer / tiger |

| er | ir | ur | | er | ir | ur |

| skirt / shirt / dirt | burn / purse / sure |

| er | ir | ur | | er | ir | ur |

Phonics IF0264   32   ©1993 Instructional Fair, Inc.

| | purse / turkey / fur | | | ruler / serve / germ |
| er | ir | ur | | ir | ur |

| | shirt / girl / chirp | | | herd / jerk / letter |
| er | | ur | | ir | ur |

| | skirt / first / third | | | hammer / tiger / ruler |
| er | | ur | | ir | ur |

| | hammer / fern / clerk | | | bird / first / girl |
| | ir | ur | | er | ur |

Phonics IF0264   33   ©1993 Instructional Fair, Inc.

Vowel Digraph oo

A new sound for you to remember today!

The letters oo in a word usually represent oo in moon (ō) or oo in book (ŏ).

moon   oo (ō)

Say the name of each picture. Circle the word. Then, circle a word that rhymes with it.

spoon / noon / to	turn / zoo / too
turtle / goose / moose	stool / duck / pool
rule / broom / tooth	moon / soon / sky

Phonics IF0264   34   ©1993 Instructional Fair, Inc.

Match these rhyming oo (ō) words.   Answers may vary.

1. moon — moo
2. shoot — spoon
3. too — boot
4. soon — moose
5. tooth — noon
6. cool — booth
7. goose — tool
8. boom — groom
9. pool — drool
10. zoo — stool
11. fool — boo

Phonics IF0264   35   ©1993 Instructional Fair, Inc.

Vowel Digraph oo (ŭ)

The second sound made by oo is the sound heard in book (ŏ).

fern   er

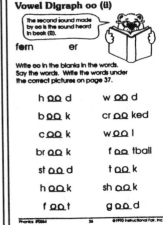

Write oo in the blanks in the words. Say the words. Write the words under the correct pictures on page 37.

h __oo__ d	w __oo__ d
b __oo__ k	cr __oo__ ked
c __oo__ k	w __oo__ l
br __oo__ k	f __oo__ tball
st __oo__ d	t __oo__ k
h __oo__ k	sh __oo__ k
f __oo__ t	g __oo__ d

Phonics IF0264   36   ©1993 Instructional Fair, Inc.

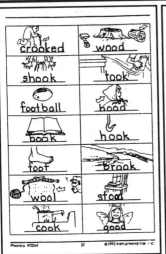

crooked | wood
shook | took
football | hood
book | hook
foot | brook
wool | stool
cook | good

Vowel Digraph au

Here's another new sound for you.

The letters **au** and **aw** make the vowel sound heard in saw and because (a).

faucet   au (a)

Write **au** in the blanks in these words.

au tomobile	f **au** cet
bec **au** se	s **au** cer
l **au** ndry	h **au** l

Answer the riddles with an **au** word from the box.

1. Your dad drives it. **automobile**

2. You turn it to get a drink. **faucet**

3. Sometimes when you ask why, your dad says, " **Because** ."

---

4. It goes with a cup. **saucer**

5. You do this when you carry trash away in a big truck. **haul**

6. When someone washes clothes, they do this. **laundry**

Read the **au** words. Draw a picture.

automobile	saucer

Vowel Digraph aw

The sound made by **aw** is the same as **er** and **ir**.

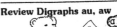

paw   aw

Write **aw** in the blanks of these words. Draw a line to the correct picture.

s **aw**
f **aw** n
l **aw** n
str **aw**
cr **aw** l
y **aw** n
aw ring
sh **aw** l
h **aw** k

Find the **aw** words from page 40 in the wordsearch. The words go → and ↓.

p	l	e	i	t	r	f	o	m	b
c	e	f	s	t	r	a	w	j	k
l	s	h	a	w	l	w	m	o	p
a	d	a	w	n	i	n	g	h	i
c	r	a	w	l	p	j	l	k	m
n	r	s	w	l	a	h	a	w	k
t	u	v	y	a	w	n	z	b	x
d	e	l	a	w	l	r	b	a	c	d
b	o	m	t	n	a	p	l	c	b
w	m	q	l	a	w	p	l	t	c

Can you also find: law, raw, paw, claw?

Review Digraphs au, aw

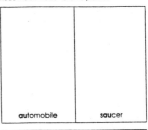
au aw

Remember that **au** and **aw** have the same sound. Read the words. Cut them out. Glue the words beside the correct pictures below and on page 43.

1. **crawl**

2. **straw**

laundry	saucer	faucet
claw	hawk	yawn
straw	fawn	awning
crawl	shawl	automobile

3. | claw
4. | automobile
5. | yawn
6. | faucet
7. | shawl
8. | laundry
9. | fawn
10. | awning
11. | saucer
12. | hawk

Vowel Digraph ea

The vowel sound **ea** doesn't always follow the rule. In this case, **ea** makes the short ĕ sound.

feather   ea

Write **ea** in the blanks in the words. Say the words. Draw a line to the correct picture.

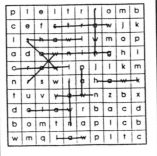

l **ea** d
br **ea** kfast
sw **ea** ter
m **ea** dow
br **ea** th
br **ea** d
w **ea** ther
d **ea** f

Read the **ea** (ĕ) words in the box. Answer the riddles with the **ea** words.

| head | sweater | weather |
| ready | leather | breath |

1. Your shoes made from animal skins are **leather** .

2. Someone tells about it on TV. **weather**

3. The top of your body. **head**

4. You wear it to keep warm. **sweater**

5. Every morning, you get **ready** for school.

6. You can see it on a cold day. **breath**

Review Vowel Digraphs

In each list, circle the word(s) with the same vowel digraph sound as found in the name of the picture.

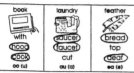

book	laundry	feather
with	saucer ⃝	bread ⃝
hood ⃝	faucet ⃝	top
cook ⃝	cut	deaf ⃝
oo (u)	ou (a)	ea (e)

Use these words to write the name of each picture.

saucer	cook
bread	faucet
hood	deaf

Phonics IF0264   46   ©1993 Instructional Fair, inc.

In each list, circle the word(s) with the same vowel digraph sound as found in the name of the picture.

spoon	fawn	breakfast
goose ⃝	crawl ⃝	weather ⃝
hood	faucet	head ⃝
boot ⃝	shawl ⃝	park
oo (u)	au (a)	ea (e)

Write these words in the correct sentences.

1. The __goose__ is white.

2. Put your hat on your __head__ .

3. The __weather__ is very cold.

4. I put my __boot__ on my foot.

5. A baby likes to __crawl__ .

6. Put the __shawl__ on your shoulders.

Phonics IF0264   47   ©1993 Instructional Fair, inc.

Diphthong ou

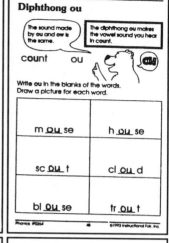

The sound made by ou and ow is the same.

The diphthong ou makes the vowel sound you hear in count.

count   ou

Write ou in the blanks of the words. Draw a picture for each word.

m __ou__ se	h __ou__ se
sc __ou__ t	cl __ou__ d
bl __ou__ se	tr __ou__ t

Phonics IF0264   48   ©1993 Instructional Fair, inc.

Write ou in these words. Say the words. Write them in the correct sentences.

sh __ou__ t   b __ou__ nce   m __ou__ th

r __ou__ nd   p __ou__ nd   pr __ou__ d

1. My dad is __proud__ of my good grades.

2. You make a lot of noise when you __shout__ .

3. The ball is __round__ .

4. I will buy a __pound__ of meat at the store.

5. __Bounce__ the ball to me.

6. Put your __mouth__ on the horn, then blow.

Phonics IF0264   49   ©1993 Instructional Fair, inc.

Diphthong ow

The sound of ow is sometimes the same as ou.

owl   ow

Write ow in the blanks of these words. Write the words under the pictures.

fl __ow__ er   t __ow__ el   sh __ow__ er

cr __ow__ n   cl __ow__ n   fr __ow__ n

frown	shower
clown	flower
towel	crown

Phonics IF0264   50   ©1993 Instructional Fair, inc.

Write ow in the words in the box. Write the correct words in the sentences.

d __ow__ n	t __ow__ er	h __ow__ l
gr __ow__ l	br __ow__ n	b __ow__

1. Remember to __bow__ after you sing the song.

2. The elevator goes up and __down__ .

3. The big dog made a loud __growl__ .

4. A tall __tower__ was up on the hill.

5. Wolves love to __howl__ .

6. Wear your good __brown__ shoes today.

Phonics IF0264   51   ©1993 Instructional Fair, inc.

Diphthong oi

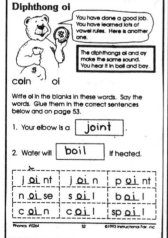

You have done a good job. You have learned lots of vowel rules. Here is another one.

The diphthongs oi and oy make the same sound. You hear it in boil and boy.

coin   oi

Write oi in the blanks in these words. Say the words. Glue them in the correct sentences below on page 53.

1. Your elbow is a __joint__ .

2. Water will __boil__ if heated.

j __oi__ nt	j __oi__ n	p __oi__ nt
n __oi__ se	s __oi__ l	b __oi__ l
c __oi__ n	c __oi__ l	sp __oi__ l

Phonics IF0264   52   ©1993 Instructional Fair, inc.

---

3. I found a very old __coin__ in the dirt.

4. The rope was placed in a neat __coil__ .

5. The __point__ of my pencil is broken.

6. The baby cried when he heard the __noise__ .

7. Put the food away so it won't __spoil__ .

8. I want to __join__ the Girl Scouts.

9. Put __soil__ in the pot.

Phonics IF0264   53   ©1993 Instructional Fair, inc.

Vowel Dipthong oy

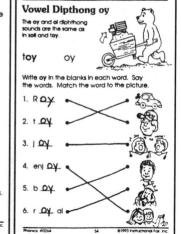

The oy and oi diphthong sounds are the same as in soil and toy.

toy   oy

Write oy in the blanks in each word. Say the words. Match the word to the picture.

1. R __oy__

2. t __oy__

3. j __oy__

4. enj __oy__

5. b __oy__

6. r __oy__ al

Phonics IF0264   54   ©1993 Instructional Fair, inc.

Panel 1 (top-left)

Work these diphthong **oy** crossword puzzles.
Use the words on page 54.

Across:
1. a man's name

Down:
2. a male child

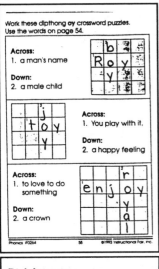

R o y (with boy down)

Across:
1. You play with it.

Down:
2. a happy feeling

t o y (joy down)

Across:
1. to love to do something

Down:
2. a crown

e n j o y (royal down)

Phonics IF0264   55   ©1993 Instructional Fair, Inc.

Panel 2 (top-middle)

Review Diphthongs oi, oy

Remember that **oi** and **oy** make the same sound, as in boil or Roy.

boil   oi
Roy   oy

Say the **oi** or **oy** names of these pictures. The **oi** or **oy** has been put in the words. You write the other letters.

r oy a l
n oi s e
c oi n
oi l

Phonics IF0264   56   ©1993 Instructional Fair, Inc.

Panel 3 (top-right)

s oy
c oi l
p oi n t
b oi l
j oi n t
b oy
t oy
s oi l

Phonics IF0264   57   ©1993 Instructional Fair, Inc.

Panel 4 (middle-left)

Diphthong ew

The sound **ew** makes can be heard in new. This is a time when w is a vowel.

The letters **ew** make a sound like long ū.

Write **ew** in the blanks of the words. Say the words. Write them in the correct sentence below and on page 59.

f ew	bl ew	ch ew
d ew	st ew	thr ew
n ew	cr ew	j ew el
n ew s	fl ew	scr ew

1. I blew a kiss to my mother.
2. The builder needed one more screw.
3. I watched the news.

Phonics IF0264   58   ©1993 Instructional Fair, Inc.

Panel 5 (middle-middle)

4. The dew made the grass very wet.
5. The pitcher threw the ball to first base.
6. Please chew your food very well.
7. Do you have new shoes?
8. The jewel in her ring was big.
9. I have only a few cents left.
10. The bird flew high in the air.
11. The man and his crew went to work.
12. I like to eat stew.

Phonics IF0264   59   ©1993 Instructional Fair, Inc.

Panel 6 (middle-right)

Review Diphthongs oi, ew

Write **oi** or **ew** in the blanks to make words. Draw a line to the correct picture.

1. n ew s
2. s oi l
3. j ew el
4. b oi l
5. c oi n
6. ch ew
7. st ew
8. p oi nt
9. n oi se
10. n ew

Phonics IF0264   60   ©1993 Instructional Fair, Inc.

Panel 7 (bottom-left)

Say the name of the picture. Circle the vowel diphthong sound.

ew (oy)   oi (ew)   ew (oi)
(oy) ew   ew (oi)   oi (ew)
(ew) oi   (oy) ew   ew (oi)
oi (ew)   (oi) ew   (oy) ew

Phonics IF0264   61   ©1993 Instructional Fair, Inc.

Panel 8 (bottom-middle)

Review ar, or

Time for a review.

ar   or

Say the name of the picture. Circle the word. Write the word.

(park) / pork — park
tarn / (torn) — torn
stark / (stork) — stork
(barn) / born — barn
star / (store) — store
(card) / cord — card

Phonics IF0264   62   ©1993 Instructional Fair, Inc.

Panel 9 (bottom-right)

Make a picture for these **ar** and **or** words. Circle **ar** or **or**.

ar		(ar)
(or)		or
horn		car
(ar)		ar
or		(or)
star		torch
ar		(ar)
(or)		or
corn		park
(ar)		ar
or		(or)
dart		fork

Phonics IF0264   63   ©1993 Instructional Fair, Inc.

Review ir, er, ur

Remember that ir, er and ur all have the same sound. They just look a little different.

More review!

ir er ur

Look at the picture. Say the name. The vowel digraphs (ir, er, ur) are given. Write the other letters. Color the pictures.

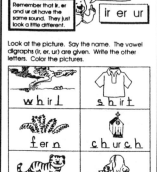

w h ir l	s h ir t
f er n	c h ur c h
t i g er	c ur l

Phonics IF0264   64   ©1993 Instructional Fair, Inc.

Choose a word to complete the sentence.

A match will — burn. / skirt.

Give money to a — herd. / clerk.

Put on a clean — shirt. / jerk.

Is your leg — curb? / hurt?

All cats have — fur. / fern.

Get in line — term. / first.

Phonics IF0264   65   ©1993 Instructional Fair, Inc.

Y as I or E

Do you remember the sounds of y?

Y = e or i

Circle I or e by each word to show its sound.

funny	ⓔ	sky	ⓘ
fly	ⓘ	puppy	ⓔ
jelly	ⓔ	fry	ⓘ
bunny	ⓔ	cry	ⓘ

Phonics IF0264   66   ©1993 Instructional Fair, Inc.

Say the words on page 66. If the y says i, write it under i. If the y says e, write it under e. If you can think of more words, write them.

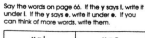

y = i	y = e
shy	candy
sky	funny
fly	puppy
fry	jelly
cry	bunny

Phonics IF0264   67   ©1993 Instructional Fair, Inc.

Review Vowel Digraph oo

Let's review oo next.

oo = ū or ŭ

moon = ū   hook = ŭ

Say the name of each picture. Circle ū or ŭ. Write the other letters of each word.

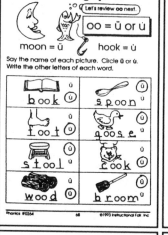

b oo k ⓤ	s p oo n Ⓤ
f oo t ⓤ	g oo s e Ⓤ
s t oo l ⓤ	c oo k ⓤ
w oo d ⓤ	b r oo m Ⓤ

Phonics IF0264   68   ©1993 Instructional Fair, Inc.

Write the oo words from page 68 in the columns. Put the ū words under moon. Put the ŭ words under hook. Add more words if you can.

oo = ū moon	oo = ŭ hook
spoon	book
goose	foot
stool	cook
broom	wood

Phonics IF0264   69   ©1993 Instructional Fair, Inc.

Review au, aw

Let's have another look at au and aw.

au aw

Say the words in the box. Find them in the wordsearch puzzle. They go → and ↓.

auto	paws	because	haul
claw	laws	saucer	yawn

p	l	t	y	a	w	n	r
b	e	c	a	u	s	e	f	h
c	b	l	u	p	a	w	s	g
w	b	a	l	a	w	s	e	j
l	k	s	a	u	c	e	r	f
p	d	m	h	t	g	n	o
r	c	s	l	d	l	a	w	s

Phonics IF0264   70   ©1993 Instructional Fair, Inc.

Use the au and aw words from page 70 in these sentences.

1. When I am 16, I will learn to drive an _auto_ .
2. The kitten licked her _paws_ .
3. Help me _haul_ the trash away.
4. The hawk picked up a mouse with his _claw_ .
5. When I am sleepy, I begin to _yawn_ .
6. Dad gave Mom a fancy cup and _saucer_ .
7. Grandma always obeys all the _laws_ .
8. My arm hurts _because_ I fell down.

Phonics IF0264   71   ©1993 Instructional Fair, Inc.

Review ou, ow

You did so well on the other reviews. Let's try ou and ow.

ou ow

Answer each question by circling yes or no.

Does a clown wear a gown?	yes / (no)
Does a cowboy ride a cow?	yes / (no)
Does an owl howl?	yes / (no)
Do you use a towel after a shower?	(yes) / no
Does a mouse have a mouth?	(yes) / no
Do you have flowers at your house?	yes / no
Does a mouse have a pouch?	yes / (no)

Phonics IF0264   72   ©1993 Instructional Fair, Inc.

Tutor's Guide IF0264   H   ©1993 Instructional Fair, Inc.

crooked

_____

_____

_____

_____

_____

_____

_____

_____

_____

_____

_____

_____

_____

Vowel Digraph au

Here's another new sound for you.

The letters **au** and **aw** make the vowel sound heard in saw and because (**a**).

faucet   au (a)

Write **au** in the blanks in these words.

<u>au</u> tomobile	f ___ cet
bec ___ se	s ___ cer
l ___ ndry	h ___ l

Answer the riddles with an **au** word from the box.

1. Your dad drives it. _____

2. You turn it to get a drink. _____

3. Sometimes when you ask why, your dad

   says, " _____ ."

4. It goes with a cup. _____

5. You do this when you carry trash away

   in a big truck. _____

6. When someone washes clothes, they

   do this. _____

Read the **au** words. Draw a picture.

automobile	s**au**cer

Vowel Digraph aw

The sound made by **aw** is the same as **au**.

paw   aw

Write **aw** in the blanks of these words.
Draw a line to the correct picture.

s ____   ●   ●

f ____ n   ●   ●

l ____ n   ●   ●

str ____   ●   ●

cr ____ l   ●   ●

y ____ n   ●   ●

____ ning   ●   ho-   ●
                        hum...

sh ____ l   ●   ●

h ____ k   ●   ●

Find the **aw** words from page 40 in the
wordsearch. The words go → and ↓.

p	l	e	i	t	r	f	o	m	b
c	e	f	s	t	r	a	w	j	k
l	s	h	a	w	l	w	m	o	p
a	d	a	w	n	i	n	g	h	i
c	r	a	w	l	p	j	l	k	m
n	r	s	w	l	a	h	a	w	k
t	u	v	y	a	w	n	z	b	x
d	c	l	a	w	r	b	a	c	d
b	o	m	t	n	a	p	l	c	b
w	m	q	l	a	w	p	l	t	c

Can you also find: law, raw, paw, claw?

Review Digraphs au, aw

Remember that **au** and **aw** have the same sound. Read the words. Cut them out. Glue the words beside the correct pictures below and on page 43.

1.

2. crawl

Vowel Digraph ea

The vowel sound **ea** doesn't always follow the rule. In this case, **ea** makes the short ĕ sound.

f**ea**ther   ea

Write **ea** in the blanks in the words. Say the words. Draw a line to the correct picture.

l____d   •   •

br____kfast •   •

sw____ter •   •

m____dow •   •

br____th •   •

br____d •   •

w____ther •   •

d____f •

Read the **ea** (ĕ) words in the box. Answer the riddles with the **ea** words.

head	sweater	weather
ready	leather	breath

1. Your shoes made from animal skins

   are _____ .

2. Someone tells about it on TV.

   _____

3. The top of your body. _____

4. You wear it to keep warm. _____

5. Every morning, you get _____

   for school.

6. You can see it on a cold day.

   _____

Review Vowel Digraphs

In each list, circle the word(s) with the same vowel digraph sound as found in the name of the picture.

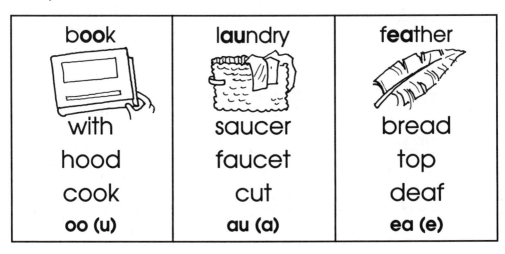

book	**lau**ndry	**fea**ther
with	saucer	bread
hood	faucet	top
cook	cut	deaf
oo (u)	**au (a)**	**ea (e)**

Use these words to write the name of each picture.

saucer _____

_____ _____

_____ _____

In each list, circle the word(s) with the same vowel digraph sound as found in the name of the picture.

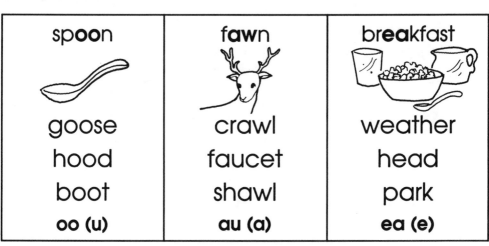

spoon	fawn	breakfast
goose	crawl	weather
hood	faucet	head
boot	shawl	park
oo (u)	**au (a)**	**ea (e)**

Write these words in the correct sentences.

1. The _____ is white.

2. Put your hat on your _____ .

3. The _____ is very cold.

4. I put my _____ on my foot.

5. A baby likes to _____ .

6. Put the _____ on your shoulders.

Diphthong ou

The sound made by **ou** and **ow** is the same.

The diphthong **ou** makes the vowel sound you hear in c**ou**nt.

c**ou**nt   ou

Write **ou** in the blanks of the words.
Draw a picture for each word.

m _ou_ se	h ___ se
sc ___ t	cl ___ d
bl ___ se	tr ___ t

Write **ou** in these words. Say the words. Write them in the correct sentences.

sh ___ t   b ___ nce   m ___ th

r ___ nd   p ___ nd   pr ___ d

1. My dad is _____ of my good

   grades.

2. You make a lot of noise when you

   _____ .

3. The ball is _____ .

4. I will buy a _____ of meat at

   the store.

5. _____ the ball to me.

6. Put your _____ on the horn,

   then blow.

Diphthong ow

The sound of **ow** is
sometimes the same as **ou**.

owl   ow

Write **ow** in the blanks of these words.   Write
the words under the pictures.

fl ___ er	t ___ el	sh ___ er
cr ___ n	cl ___ n	fr o̲w̲ n

frown

Write **ow** in the words in the box.   Write the correct words in the sentences.

d ___ n	t ___ er	h ___ l
gr ___ l	br ___ n	b ___

1. Remember to _____ after you sing the song.

2. The elevator goes up and _____ .

3. The big dog made a loud _____ .

4. A tall _____ was up on the hill.

5. Wolves love to _____ .

6. Wear your good _____ shoes today.

Diphthong oi

You have done a good job. You have learned lots of vowel rules. Here is another one.

The diphthongs **oi** and **oy** make the same sound. You hear it in b**oi**l and b**oy**.

c**oi**n   oi

Write **oi** in the blanks in these words. Say the words. Glue them in the correct sentences below and on page 53.

1. Your elbow is a [joint] .

2. Water will [   ] if heated.

j oi nt	j ___ n	p ___ nt
n ___ se	s ___ l	b ___ l
c ___ n	c ___ l	sp ___ l

3. I found a very old [_____] in the dirt.

4. The rope was placed in a neat [_____].

5. The [_____] of my pencil is broken.

6. The baby cried when he heard the [_____].

7. Put the food away so it won't [_____].

8. I want to [_____] the Girl Scouts.

9. Put [_____] in the pot.

Vowel Dipthong oy

The **oy** and **oi** diphthong
sounds are the same as
in s**oi**l and t**oy**.

toy   oy

Write **oy** in the blanks in each word. Say
the words. Match the word to the picture.

1. R oy •

•

2. t ___ •

•

3. j ___ •

•

4. enj ___ •

•

5. b ___ •

•

6. r ___ al •

•

Work these dipthong **oy** crossword puzzles.
Use the words on page 54.

Across:

1. a man's name

Down:

2. a male child

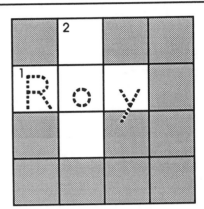

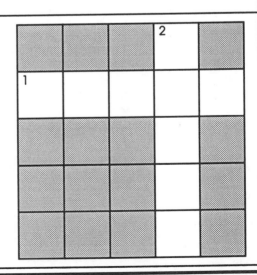

Across:

1. You play with it.

Down:

2. a happy feeling

Across:

1. to love to do something

Down:

2. a crown

Review Diphthongs oi, oy

Remember that **oi** and **oy** make the same sound, as in b**oi**l or R**oy**.

b**oi**l   **oi**

R**oy**   **oy**

Say the **oi** or **oy** names of these pictures. The **oi** or **oy** has been put in the words. You write the other letters.

___ **oy** ___ ___

___ **oi** ___ ___

___ **oi** ___

oi ___ ___

__ oy

__ oi __

__ oi __ __

__ oi __

__ oi __ __

__ oy

__ oy

__ oi __

57

Diphthong ew

The sound **ew** makes can be heard in n**ew**. This is a time when **w** is a vowel.

The letters **ew** make a sound like long **ū**.

Write **ew** in the blanks of the words. Say the words. Write them in the correct sentence below and on page 59.

f ____	bl ew	ch ____
d ____	st ____	thr ____
n ____	cr ____	j ____ el
n ____ s	fl ____	scr ____

1. I _____ a kiss to my mother.

2. The builder needed one more

   _____ .

3. I watched the _____ .

4. The _____ made the grass very wet.

5. The pitcher _____ the ball to first base.

6. Please _____ your food very well.

7. Do you have _____ shoes?

8. The _____ in her ring was big.

9. I have only a _____ cents left.

10. The bird _____ high in the air.

11. The man and his _____ went to work.

12. I like to eat _____ .

Review Diphthongs oi, ew

Write **oi** or **ew** in the blanks to make words.
Draw a line to the correct picture.

1. n e w s

2. s _ _ l

3. j _ _ el

4. b _ _ l

5. c _ _ n

6. ch _ _

7. st _ _

8. p _ _ nt

9. n _ _ se

10. n _ _

Say the name of the picture. Circle the vowel diphthong sound.

ew (oy)	oi ew	ew oi
oy ew	ew oi	oi ew
ew oi	oy ew	ew oi
oi ew	oi ew	oy ew

Review ar, or

Time for a review.

ar   or

Say the name of the picture. Circle the word.
Write the word.

park
pork

park

tarn
torn

_____

stark
stork

_____

barn
born

_____

star
store

_____

card
cord

_____

Make a picture for these **ar** and **or** words.
Circle **ar** or **or**.

ar (or) horn	ar or car
ar or star	ar or torch
ar or corn	ar or park
ar or dart	ar or fork

Review ir, er, ur

Remember that **ir**, **er** and **ur** all have the same sound. They just look a little different.

More review!

ir er ur

Look at the picture. Say the name. The vowel digraphs (ir, er, ur) are given. Write the other letters. Color the pictures.

w h ir l

__ __ ir __

__ er __

__ __ ur __ __

__ __ __ er

__ ur __

Choose a word to complete the sentence.

A match will -------	burn.
	skirt.
Give money to a	herd.
	clerk.
Put on a clean	shirt.
	jerk.
Is your leg	curb?
	hurt?
All cats have	fur.
	fern.
Get in line	term.
	first.

Y as I or E

Do you remember the sounds of **y**?

Y = e or i

Circle **i** or **e** by each word to show its sound.

funny	i / (e)	
sky	i / e	
fly	i / e	
puppy	i / e	
jelly	i / e	
fry	i / e	
bunny	i / e	
cry	i / e	

ay the words on page 66. If the **y** says **i**, write it
under **i**. If the **y** says **e**, write it under **e**. If you
can think of more words, write them.

y = i	y = e
shy	candy
_____	_____
_____	_____
_____	_____
_____	_____
_____	_____
_____	_____

Review Vowel Digraph oo

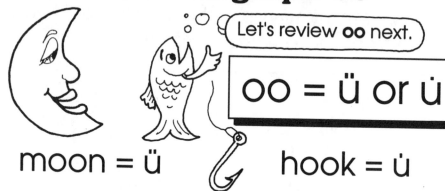

Let's review **oo** next.

$$oo = \ddot{u} \text{ or } \dot{u}$$

moon = ü   hook = u̇

Say the name of each picture. Circle **ü** or **u̇**.
Write the other letters of each word.

b oo k	ü u̇	__ __ oo __
__ oo __	ü u̇	__ __ oo __ __
__ __ oo__	ü u̇	__ oo __ __
__ oo __	ü u̇	__ __ oo __

Write the oo words from page 68 in the columns.
Put the ü words under moon. Put the ú words
under hook. Add more words if you can.

oo = ü	**oo = ú**
moon	hook
_____	_____
_____	_____
_____	_____
_____	_____
_____	_____
_____	_____

Review au, aw

Let's have another look at **au** and **aw**.

au aw

Say the words in the box. Find them in the wordsearch puzzle. They go → and ↓.

auto	paws	because	haul
claw	laws	saucer	yawn

p	l	t	h	y	a	w	n	r
b	e	c	a	u	s	e	f	h
c	b	i	u	p	a	w	s	g
w	b	c	l	a	w	s	e	j
i	k	s	a	u	c	e	r	f
p	d	m	h	t	t	g	n	o
r	c	s	l	o	l	a	w	s

se the **au** and **aw** words from page 70 in these
entences.

. When I am 16, I will learn to drive an

    _____ .

. The kitten licked her _____ .

. Help me _____ the trash away.

. The hawk picked up a mouse with his

    _____ .

. When I am sleepy, I begin to

    _____ .

. Dad gave Mom a fancy cup and

    _____ .

. Grandma always obeys all the

    _____ .

. My arm hurts _____ I fell down.

Review ou, ow

You did so well on the other reviews. Let's try **ou** and **ow**

ou ow

Answer each question by circling yes or no.

Does a clown wear a gown?	yes ~~no~~
Does a cowboy ride a cow?	yes no
Does an owl howl?	yes no
Do you use a towel after a shower?	yes no
Does a mouse have a mouth?	yes no
Do you have flowers at your house?	yes no
Does a mouse have a pouch?	yes no